W9-CHZ-234

How Things Are Made

Trees to Paper

By Inez Snyder

Children's Press®
A Division of Scholastic Inc.
New York / Toronto / London / Auckland / Sydney
Mexico City / New Delhi / Hong Kong
Danbury, Connecticut

Photo Credits: Cover © Premium Stock/Corbis; p. 5, 21 (upper left) © Stuart Westmorland/ Corbis; p. 7 © Kevin Fleming/Corbis; p. 9, 21 (upper right) © David Lees/Corbis; p. 11 © Morton Beebe/Corbis; p. 13, 15, 17, 21(lower left and lower right) © Ecoscene/Corbis; p. 19 © Nancy Sheehan/Index Stock Imagery, Inc.
Contributing Editor: Jennifer Silate
Book Design: Mindy Liu

Library of Congress Cataloging-in-Publication Data

Snyder, Inez.
    Trees to paper / by Inez Snyder.
    p. cm. — (How things are made)
    Summary: Simple words and photographs show the steps involved in making paper.
    ISBN 0-516-24264-4 (lib. bdg.) — ISBN 0-516-24356-X (pbk.)
    1. Papermaking—Juvenile literature. [1. Papermaking.] I. Title. II. Series.

TS1105.5 .S68 2003
676—dc21

2002007208

Copyright © 2003 by Rosen Book Works, Inc.
All rights reserved. Published simultaneously in Canada.
Printed in the United States of America.
1 2 3 4 5 6 7 8 9 10 R 12 11 10 09 08 07 06 05 04 03

Contents

Paper is made from trees.

The wood from the trees is cut into small **pieces**.

Water and **chemicals** are added to the wood.

This **mixture** is called **pulp**.

The pulp is put
into **machines**.

The pulp is wet.

Then, the pulp is **spread** out flat on a machine.

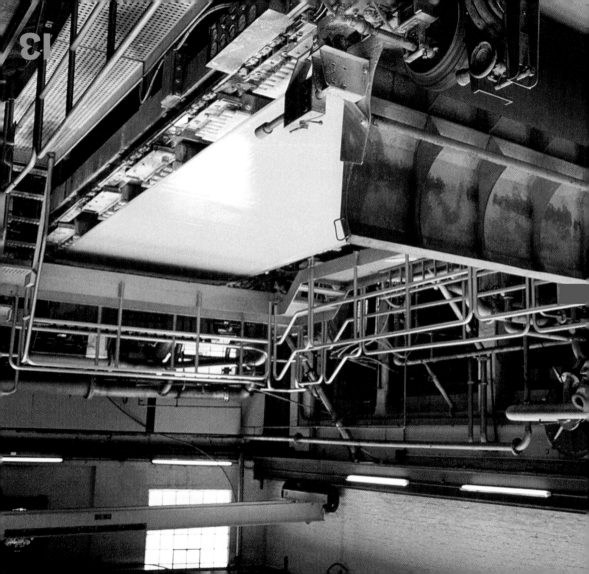

The pulp goes through many machines.

This machine dries the pulp.

The dry pulp is paper.

This machine cuts the paper into different sizes.

Paper is used for many things.

We write and draw on paper.

Many things must be done to make paper from trees.

21

New Words

chemicals (**kem**-uh-kuhlz) substances used
in chemistry
machines (muh-**sheenz**) equipment with moving
parts that are used to do a job
mixture (**miks**-chur) something that is made up of
different things mixed together
pieces (**peess**-uhz) bits of something larger
pulp (**puhlp**) a soft, wet mixture of wood
and chemicals
spread (**spred**) to unfold or stretch out

To Find Out More

Books
Paper
by Annabelle Dixon
Garrett Educational

Papermaking for Kids
by Beth Wilkinson
Gibbs Smith, Publisher

Web Site
Paper University
http://www.tappi.org/paperu
Play fun games and learn about paper and how it is made on this Web site.

Index

About the Author
Inez Snyder writes and edits children's books. She also enjoys painting and cooking for her family.

Reading Consultants
Kris Flynn, Coordinator, Small School District Literacy, The San Diego County Office of Education

Shelly Forys, Certified Reading Recovery Specialist, W.J. Zahnow Elementary School, Waterloo, IL

Sue McAdams, Former President of the North Texas Reading Council of the IRA, and Early Literacy Consultant, Dallas, TX